动植物的生活环境

Sharing the Planet | Non-Fiction Series

Copyright © 2022 by Level Learning, INC. and Washington Yu Ying PCS™
Original and Edited Text Copyright © 2022 by Washington Yu Ying PCS™

All rights reserved. No part of this book in whole or part may be reproduced without written permission from the publisher.

Published by Level Learning, INC.
Content Contributors:
Washington Yu Ying PCS™ - Aini Fang, Pearl Zao He You
Level Learning - Jingyao Qi

Illustrations by: Josh Taira

Leveling classification based on Level Learning standard.
For full description, visit www.levellearning.com

ISBN 978-1-64040-054-2
Simplified Chinese Edition

About Level Learning:
Level Learning provides a literacy focused curriculum specifically designed for K-12 Chinese as a Second Language classrooms. Our program offers 20 levels of specific and detailed objectives, leveled texts and passages, mastery-based online assessment, and analytics to enable data-driven instruction. Level Learning reading curriculum for both literature and informational text emphasize grammar and comprehension skills to help teachers develop confident and independent Chinese language readers. The non-fiction series of books are specifically designed to support our informational text course based on multiple national standards. To learn more about our entire offering, visit www.levellearning.com.

About Washington Yu Ying PCS™:
Washington Yu Ying PCS is a Mandarin English dual language immersion International Baccalaureate (IB) World school. Yu Ying's mission is to inspire and prepare young people to create a better world by challenging them to reach their full potential in a nurturing Chinese/English educational environment. Yu Ying's comprehensive IB, dual immersion curriculum equips students with global competencies for success in the real world. As a leader in immersion education, Yu Ying is determined to advance Chinese language programs and global citizenry education by helping other schools create and strengthen their Chinese programs. For more information, email: products@washingtonyuying.org

地球上有无数的动物和植物，它们生活在不同的自然环境里。

在动物和植物生活的环境里,它们可以呼吸,可以休息,可以找到食物。

仙人掌生长在沙漠。沙漠里有很多沙子,但是水很少。仙人掌可以储存水。

北极熊生活在极地。极地有很多雪和冰川,非常冷。北极熊厚厚的皮毛可以保暖。

马生活在草原上。草原上有很多草,能给马足够的食物。马还可以在草原上四处奔跑。

森林为很多动物和植物提供了很好的生存环境。比如，老虎可以躲在树林里，偷袭别的小动物。

动物和植物都生活在适合它们生长的地方。这些地方就是动物和植物的生活环境。

Glossary

	Pinyin	English Definition
地球	dì qiú	earth
动物	dòng wù	animals
植物	zhí wù	plant
生活	shēng huó	to live
自然	zì rán	natural
环境	huán jìng	environment
呼吸	hū xī	to breathe
休息	xiū xi	to rest
找	zhǎo	to find
仙人掌	xiān rén zhǎng	cactus
生长	shēng zhǎng	to grow
沙漠	shā mò	desert
储存	chǔ cún	to store
北极熊	běi jí xióng	polar bear
极地	jí dì	Arctic

	Pinyin	English Definition
冰川	bīng chuān	glacier
保暖	bǎo nuǎn	to keep warm
草原	cǎo yuán	grassland
四处	sì chù	everywhere
奔跑	bēn pǎo	to run
森林	sēn lín	forest
提供	tí gōng	to provide
躲	duǒ	to hide
偷袭	tōu xí	surprise attack
适合	shì hé	suitable

www.ingramcontent.com/pod-product-compliance
Lightning Source LLC
Chambersburg PA
CBHW041225070526
44584CB00001B/104